EGG to CHICKEN

Rachel Tonkin and Stephanie Fizer Coleman

WAYLAND
www.waylandbooks.co.uk

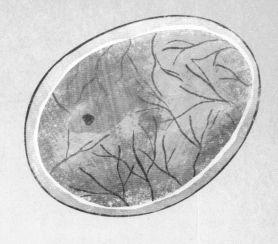

First published in Great Britain in 2019
by Wayland

Text first published in *Looking at Lifecycles*

Editor: Melanie Palmer
Designer: Lisa Peacock

HB ISBN: 978 1 5263 1025 5
PB ISBN: 978 1 5263 1026 2

Printed and bound in China

Wayland, an imprint of
Hachette Children's Group
Part of Hodder and Stoughton
Carmelite House
50 Victoria Embankment
London EC4Y 0DZ
An Hachette UK Company
www.hachette.co.uk
www.hachettechildrens.co.uk

MIX
Paper from
responsible sources
FSC® C104740

CONTENTS

Laying an egg

A female chicken is called a hen. She makes a nest with straw. She lays her eggs in a nest. Each egg has a new chicken inside it.

Inside an egg

At first the chicken inside
the egg is just a tiny dot.
It is called an embryo.
The yellow yolk in the
egg has food inside it.
This lets the embryo grow.

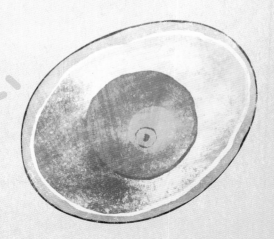

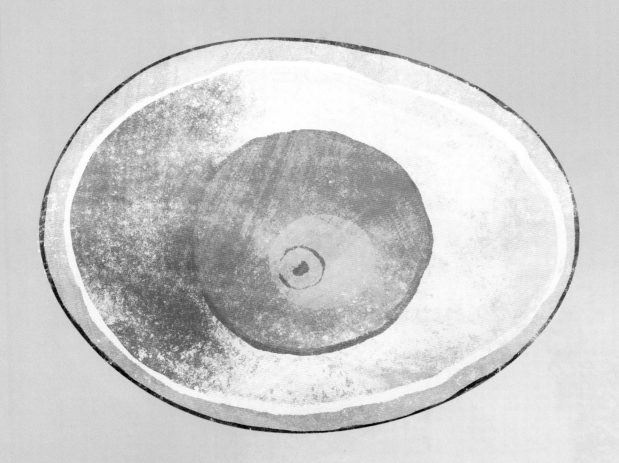

Brooding

The hen helps the embryo to grow by sitting on the eggs. She keeps them warm and safe. This is called brooding.

The embryo grows

As the embryo grows it begins to look like a chick. It is protected by a soft, jelly substance called albumen. Like the yolk, this has food in it.

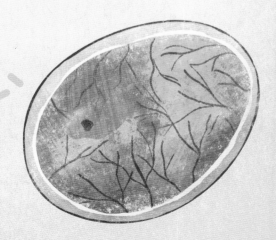

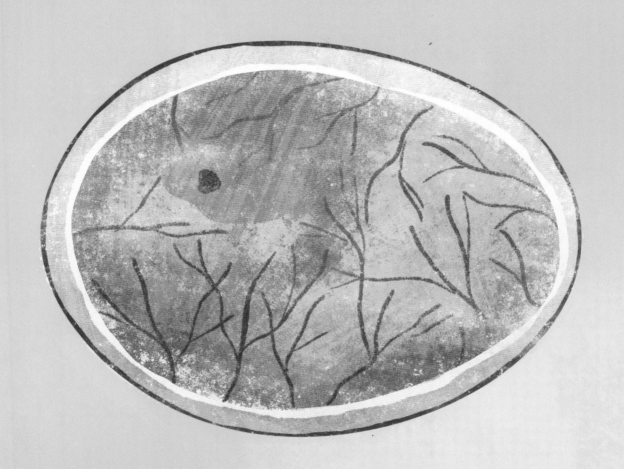

Hatching

After three weeks the chick is ready to hatch. It uses a special tooth on its beak called an egg tooth to break out of the egg.

New chick

The chick soon dries out.
It has fluffy yellow feathers,
called down. The chick
can walk as soon as
it hatches.

Growing up

As the chick gets older it grows new feathers. It starts to look like an adult chicken.

Adulthood

In a few months the chick is fully grown. Chickens peck the ground looking for food, such as seeds and worms.

Making a nest

When a female chicken is about five months old, she is ready to lay eggs and have chicks of her own.

21

Chicken life cycle

1 The hen lays her eggs in a nest.

2 Inside the egg the chick is a tiny dot called an embryo.

4 Albumen forms inside the egg to protect the chick as it grows.

3 The hen helps the embryo grow by sitting on it.

7 The chick grows feathers and starts to look like a chicken.

8 The chick is fully grown. After five months it can lay eggs of its own.

5 After three weeks the chick breaks out of the egg.

6 The new chick can walk as soon as it hatches.

Chicken facts

There are many different types of chicken. They can be different sizes and colours.

Only eggs that have been fertilised by a cockerel (male chicken) will hatch into chicks. The eggs we eat do not have a chick inside them.

It takes a chicken about 24 hours to make one egg.

Chickens can lay between 250 and 300 eggs every year.

Chickens eat insects, worms, slugs, seeds and other things they find in the ground.

Chickens can live for as long as seven years.

Chicken quiz

Test your new knowledge with this chicken life cycle quiz by answering the questions below.

Question 1
Where does the hen lay her eggs?

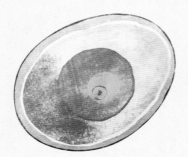

Question 2
What is inside each egg?

Question 3
Why does the hen sit on her eggs?

Question 4
How long does it take for a chick to develop inside an egg?

Question 5
What is an egg tooth?

Question 6
What colour is the chick when it hatches?

Question 7
What do adult chickens eat?

Question 8
How old is a hen when she can lay eggs of her own?

If you were a bird ...

If you were a bird, where would you like to build your nest?

High in a tree?

On a roof top?

On the beach?

On the ground?

In a hole in a tree?

In a hedge?

On a cliff?

On a window sill?

Now draw a picture of your bird on its nest.

Chick collage

What you will need:
- Pencil • A4 Sheet of card • Scissors
- Orange paper •Orange felt-tip pen
- Googly eye • Yellow feathers (from craft shop) • Glue and spreader

1. Draw the outline of a chick on the card. If you want a picture to copy, turn to p14 of this book.

2. Cut out the picture you have drawn.

3. Cut out a small triangle of orange paper and stick it onto the beak.

4. Use an orange felt-tip pen to colour in the legs.

5. Spread glue over the body of the chick and stick yellow feathers all over the body and head.

6. Glue a googly eye onto the head.

Which of these animals lays eggs?

A crocodile?

A frog?

A rabbit?

An ant?

A butterfly?

A turtle?

Answer: All of them, except the rabbit.

Chicken words

Albumen
The white part of the egg which protects the chick as it is growing.

Brooding
When a hen keeps her eggs warm by sitting on them.

Egg
Contains the baby chicken, surrounded by yolk and albumen.

Egg tooth
A tiny tooth-like point on the tip of a chick's beak. The chick uses the egg tooth to break out of the egg.

Embryo
The early stage of a young animal when it is growing inside an egg or its mother.

Feathers
The soft, light and often colourful covering of birds.

Fertilised
When an egg has a baby chick inside. This only happens when a hen and cockerel have mated.

Nest
A hollow place built or used by a bird as a home to rear its young.

Yolk
The yellow part of the egg which contains food for the chick.

Index

QUIZ ANSWERS: 1 In a nest; **2** An embryo, a yolk and albumen (egg white); **3** The hen helps her eggs grow by keeping them warm; **4** Three weeks; **5** A special tooth that a chick uses to break out of the eggshell; **6** Yellow; **7** Seeds and worms; **8** About five months old.